Common Wildflowers
of Grand Teton National Park

Written by
Charles Craighead

Photography by
Henry H. Holdsworth

**Official Guidebook
of Grand Teton National Park**

Published by
Grand Teton Natural History Association

Table *of* Contents

Wildflowers   4

Park Geology, Flowers, and the Natural
Communities   6

White Flowers   10

Yellow Flowers   18

Pink and Red Flowers   28

Blue and Purple Flowers   38

Berries and Their Flowers   46

Best Short Walks for Wildflowers   50
Death Canyon Trailhead to Phelps Lake Overlook,
East Shore of Jenny Lake, Taggart Lake Loop, and
Cascade Canyon

Selected Weeds and Nonnative Flowers   52

Index and Checklist   54

Showy Fleabane

Wildflowers

Sheer mountain peaks, pristine lakes, and abundant wildlife help define the vast scope of Grand Teton National Park, but the park's wildflowers add their own subtle element to the landscape. From the banks of the Snake River to the upper slopes of the highest peaks, hundreds of wildflower species thrive here, and every year they put on their seasonal displays of color. They appear as the winter snow first melts, and a few still dot the hillsides when the first autumn frost arrives. Blooms range from entire meadows of waist-high flowers to single, dwarf alpine plants requiring a magnifying lens to identify.

Each flowering season varies in its duration, intensity, and most prominent species, but certain wildflowers appear faithfully every year. These "common" wildflowers often line the trails through conifer forests, mark the streams and springs in the foothills, or highlight meadows in the mountain canyons. This book includes not only these common flowers, but some of the less abundant species which show up regularly in the frequently visited areas of the park. While common names for wildflowers vary from place to place, the scientific names do not. Both names are provided here for accuracy in identification and for further study.

Wildflower guidebooks rely on the observations of the reader to narrow down the possibilities, and for that reason flower color remains the primary characteristic for separating the species. Size, shape, and other physical features then help the reader sort through the choices. Other distinctions such as location, abundance, and flowering season tend to be secondary, more variable factors for identification.

Identifying flowers by name is just the beginning. Part of the appeal of wildflower identification is discovering new patterns to the blooms, watching for "old friends" to appear each season, and learning more about the complex natural systems of Grand Teton National Park. For those visitors interested in pursuing some of the more elusive wildflowers or venturing into the high country during the spectacular alpine season, comprehensive plant and wildflower identification books are available at the park's visitor centers.

Harebell (right)

Lupine near Pilgrim Creek

Park Geology, Flowers, and the Natural Communities

Soon after the glaciers of the last Ice Age melted away, 10,000 to 20,000 years ago, plants began to find their way back into the scoured valley, some carried on the wind and others slowly spreading from surrounding high country that escaped the massive ice flows. Over time, the landscape and the plant communities of the Tetons evolved together, with the plants taking root wherever they could survive. One look at the Tetons today reveals three major geologic features: the flat valley floor, the low hills and canyons, and the peaks and high country. Some obvious differences in their capability of supporting plant life can be seen: the moraines are forested; the valley is a plain of sagebrush; the waterways are clearly marked by tall trees; and high in the mountains everything gives way to bare rock.

Today there exists a number of distinct natural communities, named for their predominant type of vegetation. Each of these living communities ultimately reflects the underlying geology—the rocks, soil, water, and exposure to sunlight and wind—that shapes the park. These physical factors help set the environmental limits for plants and determine the species that can survive. The communities include sagebrush, meadow, aspen, Lodgepole Pine, spruce-fir, and alpine. Ecologists define more communities, and in much more detail than we need here, but these are useful for finding and identifying wildflowers.

Although these clearly defined natural communities exist, many exceptions to the rules also apply. This is especially true when it comes to the wildflowers inhabiting the park. In general, different plants tend to live in the different communities, but there is much overlap, with some hardy species such as dandelions surviving in a variety of places from the valley floor to high in the mountains. Other flowering plants live only in specific soil or moisture conditions, but those conditions may occur within several general communities. Thus, a wetland monkeyflower found along the broad path of the Snake River may also grow in a tiny pocket of spring-fed marsh in one of the mountain canyons.

The sagebrush community covers most of the broad, flat valley floor. It extends from the base of the mountains to the eastern border of the park and from Jackson Lake to the southern park boundary. This is dry, well-drained land with little topsoil. Wildflowers include the early blooming Spring Beauty, Sagebrush Buttercup, Steershead, and Yellow Bell. Later blooms include Arrowleaf Balsamroot and Mules-ear Wyethia.

Meadows vary from expansive fields in the valley to small open sites perched high in the canyons, but all tend to have moist soil, lots of sunlight, and a variety of grasses and flowers. Meadow wildflowers include Yampah and Blue Camas.

The aspen community mingles with others and grows in places where better soil and more water combine. Many of the small draws in the sagebrush community have aspen stands. Wildflowers here may include Sticky Geranium, One-Flower Helianthella, and Showy Fleabane.

Most of the park's conifer forests aren't purely one species, but show a mix of several kinds of trees. The Lodgepole Pine community covers the moraines that enclose places like Jenny Lake and Taggart Lake, mixing with spruce-fir as it extends along much of the base of the Tetons. Silver Lupine and Engelmann Aster grow in clearings, with Highbush Huckleberry and other shrubs preferring the open shade.

The spruce-fir community, a combination of Engelmann Spruce and Subalpine Fir, favors the moraines and the lower mountain slopes. It continues up to join Whitebark and Limber pines toward treeline. Since this forest tends to be cool and shaded, it harbors wildflowers like the Calypso Orchid and Mountain Bog Gentian. Further up, there may be clematis or paintbrush growing where the stands of trees open up into meadows.

The alpine community starts where the trees can no longer grow and continues to the highest elevations of the park. Little soil combined with lots of wind and sun limit plant life here. Alpine wildflowers are some of the hardiest, and also some of the most beautiful, in the park. Alpine species include Mountain Townsendia and the official park flower, the Alpine Forget-Me-Not.

Colorado Columbine (overleaf)

White Flowers

White Bog-orchid *Habenaria dilatata (Orchid family)*

The small, waxy, pure white flowers cluster on the upper part of spike-like stems. The lower petal is larger and hangs down, with a long spur in the back. Their narrow, pointed leaves are bright green and grow on the lower part of the 1 to 2 foot tall spike. White Bog-orchids inhabit shaded streambanks or sunlit, swampy areas.

Ladies Tresses *Spiranthes romanzoffiana (Orchid family)*

Similar at first look to White Bog-orchid, Ladies Tresses has flowers forming a spiral as they grow around the stem. There may be 50 or 60 individual flowers. The plant is about 8 to 10 inches tall, and grows in wet areas from the valley up into the lower canyons. It usually appears late in the summer.

Many-flowered Phlox *Phlox multiflora (Phlox family)*

The symmetrical blossoms of this bright, clustered plant grow in dense mats that may be up to several meters across. On close inspection each ¾ inch wide flower has a short tube expanding into the five lobes of the blossom. Phlox appears early in the season on dry ridges and hills and among sagebrush.

Sego Lily *Calochortus eurycarpos (Lily family)*

The Sego Lily produces its white blossom on the end of a stem anywhere from 10 to 20 inches tall. Three large petals, each with a purple spot, and three narrow, green sepals identify it. Sego Lilies grow on the sagebrush flats and on dry hillsides. They have edible roots that were widely used by American Indians.

Yampah *Perideridia gairdneri (Carrot family)*

Yampah is a slender-stalked plant 1 to 3 feet tall, with small white flowers in branched clusters at the top. Individually the plants are fairly nondescript, but they usually grow in abundance and can fill a meadow or open hillside. Yampah roots are a favorite food of bears and were a staple food of the Native Americans of the region.

Common Yarrow *Achillea millefolium (Composite family)*

Yarrow grows 1 to 3 feet tall with a flat-topped cluster of tiny white flowers, each only about an eighth-inch across. The flower stems branch off the main stem at different heights but all end up more or less at the same level. The leaves appear almost fern-like and get progressively smaller toward the top. Yarrow was used by American Indians as a medicine.

Cowparsnip *Heracleum sphondylium (Parsley family)*

This tall, coarse plant with a cluster of small flowers at the top grows up to 8 feet tall with umbels that can be a foot across. Most plants range from 3 to 5 feet high, with flower clusters about six inches wide. The leaves are very large, especially at the base of the plant. Many animals, including elk and bears, eat cowparsnip.

Woodland Strawberry *Fragaria vesca (Rose family)*

These easily-recognized little wildflowers are found in low, spreading bunches in moist soil along streams, in the open woods, and in meadows. The flowers each exhibit five white, rounded petals. Wild strawberries look like small versions of cultivated ones, but are generally sweeter and more flavorful.

White Flowers, continued

Thimbleberry *Rubus parviflorus (Rose family)*

The Thimbleberry flower looks somewhat like other roses with its five round, white petals, but the Thimbleberry plant grows up to 6 feet high. Its thornless stems separate it from raspberry. The flowers are up to 1.5 inches across, and the leaves can be 8 inches wide. Thimbleberry grows along streams in the foothills and lower canyons, especially in the shade of aspen trees.

White Mules Ear *Wyethia helainthoides (Composite Family)*

Growing in moist meadows in the northern park, this large flower is hard to miss. Two feet high, with flowers up to 4 inches across, it appears in June. It has large, lance-shaped leaves both at the base and on the stem. Like the more common yellow Mules-ear, it grows in large clusters with blossoms that tend to face the sun.

Mountain Death Camas *Zigadenus elegans (Lily family)*

The early-blooming Death Camas gets its name from the poisonous alkaloids it contains. It is often mistaken for the edible true camas. Death Camas prefers meadows and sage flats, reaching a foot or two in height. It has a cluster of small flowers at the end of each stem and long, grass-like leaves at the base. Like other lilies, each flower has three small petals and three sepals.

Sulfur Buckwheat *Erigonum umbellatum (Buckwheat family)*

Buckwheat flowers grow in an umbrella-shaped cluster on an almost leafless 12-inch stem. The leaves are usually in a dense mat on the ground. The sulfur yellow flowers bloom in large numbers where they occur and are common in dry soil in the sagebrush flats. The flowers may be creamy white in places, with hints of red as they age.

Showy Green Gentian *Frasera speciosa (Gentian family)*

The whitish-green flowers of this plant are only noticeable on close inspection, but they are striking. The 2 to 5 foot tall Green Gentian stands out in a grass or sagebrush meadow. Its numerous small flowers grow on stalks branching off the upper part of the plant. This plant lives many years as a low circle of leaves before it sends up its flowering spike and then dies.

False Solomon Seal *Smilacina racemosa (Lily family)*

These delicate looking flowers grow on the end of an unbranched stem about 2 to 3 feet tall. Large leaves sprout all the way up the stem, with 2 to 4 inch long flower clusters at the end. They usually grow in moist, shaded areas near lakes or streams. The reddish berries are edible but are similar in appearance to poisonous baneberries.

Englemann Aster *Aster engelmannii (Composite family)*

A number of daisy-looking flowers grow in the park, but this has a yellow disk flower in the center, with 9 to 15 thin, white petals around it. Each petal extends about an inch, and bent or missing petals often give the flower a ragged look. The leaves are lance-shaped, with the largest ones in the middle of the plant. Look for it in the moist soil of the shaded forest.

Marsh Marigold *Caltha leptosepala (Buttercup family)*

This white flower shows up in canyon meadows as the snow is first melting. The bright blossoms grow low to the ground in a bed of thick, shiny leaves and are about 1 to 2 inches across. It doesn't have true petals, but has up to 12 white petal-like sepals, and the leaves are not lobed. Elk will eat it as they first move into the high country for the summer.

White Flowers, continued

Colorado Columbine *Aquilegia coerulea (Buttercup family)*

This beautiful columbine grows in wet or moist soil in shaded areas, and its 1 to 2 foot height often makes it stand out. The delicate flowers are 1 to 3 inches across, with five white sepals and a long spur extending from the base of each of the 5 petals. There is little chance of confusing this flower with another species.

Rocky Mountain Parnassia *Parnassia fimbriata (Saxifrage family)*

A unique little flower of wet areas along streams and lake shores, Parnassia grows 6 to 12 inch tall stems with a single flower. Fringed edges of the 5 white petals and ten alternating stamens, five white and five yellow, identify it. The parnassia plant has heart-shaped leaves on long stalks at the base and a single bract-like leaf on the main stem.

Northern Bedstraw *Galium boreale (Madder family)*

Bedstraw is recognized by its small, saucer-like flowers and a 4-sided stem. The plant rises about 1 to 2 feet tall, with the leaves in whorls of four and tiny white hairs that will catch on clothing. Bedstraw grows in moist soil in the forest. The Madder family includes the coffee plant, and the seeds of bedstraw have been used like coffee beans.

American Bistort *Polygonum bistortoides (Buckwheat family)*

Bistort has a cluster of tiny flowers forming a white tuft at the top of its 1 to 2 foot tall stem and narrow, tapered leaves. From a distance a meadow full of bistort looks like little tufts of swaying cotton. It grows along stream banks and in wet meadows in the mountains early in the summer. Bears and rodents eat the snake-like root.

White Campion *Silene latifolia (Pink Family)*

Even though this flower is not native to the park, it has been here a long time and is common along the roadways. White Campion has male and female flowers on separate plants. A key feature is a ring of petal-like flaps inside the petals, around the opening to the corolla tube.

Tufted Evening Primrose *Oenthera cespitosa*
(Evening Primrose family)

The Evening Primrose is a large, stemless flower growing in a bed of leaves in dry, open ground. The 2-inch wide blossoms slowly turn from white to pink as they age. This flower is short-lived and first opens its blossom in the evening. During the day it wilts or closes.

White Dryas *Dryas octopetala (Rose family)*

This small, low plant of the mountains produces a large white flower with 8 to 10 petals. The leathery, toothed evergreen leaves form a thick mat. The stem is stout and woody, with a single blossom. This plant is well adapted to withstand the windy and dry conditions of life at high elevations.

Snowbrush Ceanothus *Ceanothus velutinus*
(Buckthorn family)

A low shrub growing on the moraines and foothills of the mountains, Snowbrush has bright, shiny evergreen leaves and large clusters of small white flowers. The plant is about 2 to 5 feet high. Common on open hillsides close to the mountains, Snowbrush is especially suited to areas that have burned in a wildfire.

Butter and Eggs (overleaf)

Yellow Flowers

Arrowleaf Balsamroot *Balsamorhiza sagittata* *(Composite family)*

Balsamroot grows in large, conspicuous bunches nearly 2 feet tall and often covers entire meadows or hillsides in early summer. It is one of the most noticeable flowers in the park. The bright yellow flowers erupt on long leafless stems rising out of a clump of arrowhead-shaped leaves. There is one flower per stalk, and the leaves are covered with fine, silvery hairs.

Mules-ear Wyethia *Wyethia amplexicaulis (Composite family)*

Mules-ear blooms on the heels of balsamroot and is often mistaken for it, but this plant has shiny, dark green leaves and up to five yellow flowers on each stalk. Also, the mule-ear-shaped leaves grow all along the flower stem. In certain parts of the park there is a closely related white-flowered species (page 12).

Low Hawksbeard *Crepis modocensis (Composite family)*

Hawksbeard looks somewhat like a mountain dandelion, but the Hawksbeard has leaves growing from the stem and fewer petals. It produces ray flowers only, with no disk in the center. The plant exhibits a light appearance from a coat of fine yellowish hairs and, if accidentally broken, seeps a milky juice. Hawksbeard inhabits dry, open places.

Mountain Dandelion *Agoseris glauca (Composite family)*

Similar to a common dandelion, this plant can reach nearly two feet in height. The flowers grow up to 1.5 inches across and have no center disk. The leaves all grow at the base. Mountain Dandelions contain a milky sap that turns rubbery when exposed to air. It was chewed like gum by some American Indians.

One-flower Helianthella *Helianthella uniflora*
(Aster family)

Helianthella looks like a sunflower, but it has a single flower with a light center disk and grows on a 1 to 4 foot tall stem. It usually blooms in small clusters, with flower heads from 1.5 to 2.5 inches across. Its lower leaves are opposite each other and upper ones alternate. Helianthella grows in moist meadows, especially in the open shade of aspen trees near water.

Sagebrush Buttercup *Ranunculus glaberrimus*
(Buttercup family)

There are a dozen buttercup species in the park, but this one blooms very early in the season, soon after the snow melts. It is common in the sagebrush flats of the park. The bright, shiny yellow flower grows close to the ground. This is the only buttercup with two kinds of leaves, ones that are whole and ones that are lobed.

Yellow Violet *Viola nuttallii (Violet family)*

These delicate, bright yellow violets appear in late spring when snow melts and the soil is still moist. They look like small, yellow pansies with lance-shaped leaves. The violet has five petals, with the lowest one containing nectar, and are common in sagebrush areas.

Desert Parsley *Lomatium foeniculaceum (Carrot Family)*

Also called biscuit root, Desert Parsley is a coarse, 1 to 4 foot tall plant with large umbrella-shaped clusters of small, yellowish flowers. It has large leaves that are deeply split three or four times and look like parsley or carrot tops. It blooms in spring and early summer in dry, rocky soil. Many wild species in this family have edible roots and were used by Native Americans for food.

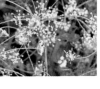

Yellow Flowers, continued

Rabbitbrush *Chrysothamnus nauseosus (Composite family)*

Park roadsides and turnouts are often framed by thick bunches of this yellow-flowered shrub in late summer. A ragged brush with light green stems and very slender gray-green leaves, Rabbitbrush grows in dry soil and is often mixed in with sagebrush. It was used medicinally by Native Americans.

Shrubby Cinquefoil *Potentilla fruiticosa (Rose family)*

This cinquefoil is a 1 to 5 foot tall shrub with many branches and small, thick, year-round leaves. It produces bright yellow flowers, each about ¾ inch across, and reddish-brown bark hanging loosely from the stems. Cinquefoil grows in damp soil along streams, where its blooms may last for most of the summer.

Prairie Coneflower *Ratibida columnifera (Aster Family)*

A fairly recent arrival from the plains and prairies, the coneflower is unmistakable. The flower's disk forms a large, dark brown cone with just a few yellow petals that hang down. The cone may not be evident until later in the summer. Native Americans brewed a medicinal tea from the coneflower heads.

Nodding Little Sunflower *Helianthella quinquenervis (Aster family)*

Found growing on moraines near the base of the mountains, this sunflower-like plant blooms in mid to late summer. It can grow to 5 or 6 feet tall, with large flowers that are 3 to 4 inches across. Its petals are pale yellow rather than the bright yellow of true sunflowers, the center disk is yellow, and each leaf has five prominent veins.

Heartleaf Arnica *Arnica cordifolia (Composite family)*

Arnica, a single-stemmed flower growing in open Lodgepole or aspen forests, has a blossom about two inches across. The stem reaches 8 to 24 inches tall. This flower gets its name from its elongated, heart-shaped leaves, which grow opposite each other on the stem. This species and other arnicas are important sources of herbal medicines.

Wooly Daisy *Eriophyllum lanatum (Composite family)*

This flower is not a true daisy, but resembles one. Fine white hairs cover the leaves to help prevent water loss. It grows in clumps about 1 to 1.5 feet high, with numerous daisy-like flowers about ¾ of an inch to an inch wide. Eriophyllum inhabits dry soil on the sagebrush flats and moraines.

Showy Goldeneye *Viguiera multiflora (Composite family)*

This sunflower-looking plant blooms late, after most of the similar yellow flowers have gone to seed. The center of the flower is enlarged and rounded instead of being flat like a sunflower. Several secondary stems of the 1 to 4 foot tall plant branch off from one. Look for it in dry soil near the mountains and in the hills of the eastern part of the park.

Western Groundsel *Senecio integerrimus (Composite family)*

Groundsel differs from the many yellow flowers in the park by its single stem with a cluster of flowers branching off at the top and the central flower usually being the lowest of the bunch. The plant is about 1 to 2 feet tall, and grows in gravel or sand on the valley floor. It produces toxins poisonous to horses and cattle.

Yellow Flowers, continued

Blazing Star Mentzelia *Mentzelia laevicaulis (Blazing star family)*

A large, unmistakable flower with five petals and a thick cluster of yellow stamens, Mentzelia blossoms close during the day but at morning and evening may open to 4 inches across. Blazing Star grows in dry, sandy or gravelly soil, and its leaves are covered with barbed hairs that stick to clothing.

Yellow Bell *Fritillaria pudica (Lily family)*

A small and delicate early summer flower, Yellow Bell grows in moist ground soon after the snow melts. It is common in sagebrush meadows along the base of the mountains. The single bell shaped flowers hang down from the end of the stems, which are only about 3 to 8 inches tall. The flowers gradually turn dull red as they age. The root is dug up by bears and rodents in the spring.

Yellow Columbine *Aquilegia flavescens (Buttercup family)*

This is a familiar looking columbine with a long spur-like tube extending from each of the five petals, and five showy yellow sepals. Columbines grow in moist meadows in subalpine areas along streams and on steep banks. The leaves are divided into small segments.

Rocky Mountain Pondlily *Nuphar polysepalum (Waterlily family)*

Easily identified by its location, which is most often on beaver ponds or the edges of small lakes, pondlily has large, shiny leaves lying flat on the water and big, waxy yellow flowers. The leaves grow up to a foot long, and the flowers can be three inches across. Native Americans collected and ate the Pondlily seeds.

Leopard Lily *Fritillaria atropurpurea (Lily family)*

Actually a dull, purple-brown flower, Leopard Lily's yellowish spots make it noticeable. Broad, 1-inch flowers hang down from the stem in groups of up to four. Long, narrow leaves sprout from the entire length of the stem. Leopard Lily grows in grassy meadows or in open forest and puts off a strong, unpleasant odor.

Yellow Monkeyflower *Mimulus guttatus (Figwort family)*

The Yellow Monkeyflower is common along the many small streams of the Tetons. Its bright yellow flowers are irregular, like snapdragons, and have two upper and three lower petals. Red spots on the petals help to attract insect pollinators. The size of the plant varies with location, but it may be two to three feet tall at lower elevations.

Glacier Lily *Erythronium grandiflorum (Lily family)*

Glacier Lily has lots of common names, most often called the Dogtooth Violet. The large flowers hang down from stems about 8 to 12 inches tall and appear even as the snow is melting in the spring. The petals re-curve toward the base of the flower to reveal the long stamens. The plant grows two large, shiny basal leaves.

Largeflower Hymenoxys *Hymenoxys grandiflora (Composite family)*

Hymenoxys, the mountain sunflower, inhabits rocky, limestone slopes above treeline. It stands out in the rugged terrain with its bright, 3-inch diameter flowers, and in favorable soil it grows in large numbers. The flowers orient to face east, toward the rising sun, but they do not track the sun as it moves across the sky.

Yellow Flowers, continued

Lanceleaved Stonecrop *Sedum lanceolatum*
(Stonecrop family)

Stonecrops produce thick, succulent leaves and stems, and they usually grow among the rocks or in rocky soil. This species gets its name from the clusters of numerous, pointed leaves at the base of the plant. The late-blooming flowers appear on the ends of short stems, with four or five narrow and sharply pointed petals.

Western St. Johnwort *Hypericum formosum*
(St. Johnwort family)

A high elevation plant growing in moist areas of the upper canyons, St. Johnwort produces flowers at the top of long stems with sets of opposite leaves. The blossoms have five large yellow petals, but the unopened flower buds are red. Western St. Johnwort is related to the European varieties used in traditional medicine.

Sulfur Paintbrush *Castilleja sulphurea* (Figwort family)

Indian Paintbrush is well known in the park, but this yellow species is much less common and inhabits the upper canyons and high meadows. Soft yellow bracts surround and hide the real flower. Like other paintbrushes, this one lives in part by parasitic attachment to the roots of other plants.

Please Don't Pick the Flowers

Wildflowers are one of the park's fragile resources, and it is against regulations to pick or damage any of them. Besides leaving them in place for the next hiker to see, it is also important that they be allowed to mature and go to seed. Some wildflowers, though they may seem abundant, are rare and found only in a few sites in the park.

Showy Goldeneye (right), Moss Campion (overleaf)

Pink and Red Flowers

Spring Beauty *Claytonia lanceolata (Purslane family)*

Spring Beauties appear soon after the winter snow melts and are usually gone from the valley before summer arrives. Petals vary from pink to white, but their veins remain pink. These are low plants, seldom more than 6 to 8 inches tall, with two lance-shaped leaves at the base of the stem. Grizzly bears dig up and eat the nutritious roots.

Sticky Geranium *Geranium viscosissimum (Geranium family)*

This common wildflower is found in open woods or sagebrush meadows. Later in the season it persists on cool, north facing slopes. Plants grow from 1 to 2 feet tall, usually in clumps. The one-inch flowers have five petals ranging in color from pink to lavender, with dark red veins. Sticky geranium is an important food for deer and elk in the late spring.

Wild Rose *Rosa woodsii (Rose family)*

Wild Rose grows all over the park, especially along trails and near streams in the lower elevations. The rose bush reaches 3 to 6 feet in height, with thorny stems. Flowers usually grow on fresh side stems branching off the main one, with five-petaled blossoms up to 2 inches across. Its fruit is the rose hip, an important wildlife food through the winter.

Prairiesmoke *Geum triflorum (Rose family)*

Prairiesmoke, also known as Long-plumed Avens and Grandfather's Beard, is about 1 to 2 feet tall with flowers that nod over and hang down. The hairy leaves grow mostly at the base of the plant, and they appear fern-like. It grows in open meadows and hillsides. Long, feathery styles adorn the seeds and carry them on the wind.

Longleaf Phlox *Phlox longifolia (Phlox family)*

Longleaf Phlox is similar-looking to the White Phlox also found in the park but has noticeably longer petals and long leaves. It also grows upright instead of forming a mat, and the flowers are larger and various shades of pink. In other areas the petals may be white. Longleaf Phlox grows mostly in the sagebrush areas, in gravelly soil.

Mountain Hollyhock *Iliamna rivularis (Mallow family)*

This spike-like flowering plant looks much like a cultivated hollyhock. The plant is 3 to 6 feet tall with large leaves that look like those of the maple. It grows in large clumps, preferring roads and streams. Flowers mature from the bottom of the spike upwards, with blossoms up to 2 inches across. Inside the flower, the stamens fuse together to form a tube.

Steershead *Dicentra uniflora (Bleeding-heart family)*

This rare little flower is a prized find for wildflower enthusiasts. Each single flower grows on top of a short, 2 to 4 inch leafless stem, and they range from white to pink. Steershead gets its name from its uniquely shaped flower, with two of its petals curling back to form the "horns" of the steer. The tiny flowers, about ½ inch across, appear briefly in late spring.

Shooting Star *Dodecathion conjugens (Primrose family)*

The Shooting Star's distinct shape, formed by the petals flaring backwards to reveal a dark point made of fused stamens, gives it the name. The flowers aim earthward, growing in small clusters at the top of single, 4 to 10 inch stems. Shooting stars appear not long after the snow melts, and prefer the sagebrush flats and low moraines of the park.

Pink and Red Flowers, continued

Calypso Orchid *Calypso bulbosa (Orchid family)*

Also commonly known as Fairyslipper, this beautiful little orchid grows in the cool, shaded parts of the forest during the first few weeks of summer. It is the only pink, single-flowered orchid here and usually sprouts from mossy, rotten wood on the forest floor. Only one egg-shaped leaf grows at the base of the plant.

Northern Twinflower *Linnaea borealis (Honeysuckle family)*

Twinflower forms a low, evergreen mat with short leafless branches displaying pairs of tiny, pinkish flowers. The bell-shaped flowers have a pleasant fragrance. Twinflower grows in moist areas around ponds and along streams and prefers the shade. It was the favorite flower of Carl Linnaeus, the Swedish botanist responsible for the scientific system of naming plants and animals.

Parry Primrose *Primula parryi (Primrose family)*

Primrose grows in the mountains, and its 6 to 12 inch-high flowering stems stand out with their vivid blossoms. The flowers spread out in a bunch at the top of the stems, with 3 to 12 flowers per bunch. Primrose, with its relatively large size and strong, rank odor instead of a sweet fragrance, is easy to identify.

Northern Sweetvetch *Hedysarum boreale (Pea family)*

Sweetvetch inhabits dry rocky soil in the canyons and lower mountain slopes. It grows from 1 to 2 feet tall, with clusters of flowering stems growing from one root. The flowers are each about ¼ inch long and grow in thick racemes. Sweetvetch roots were eaten by American Indians, and the seed pods are a favorite of rodents.

Alpine Laurel *Kalmia microphyllla (Heath family)*

Alpine Laurel grows on the lakeshores and along streams in the mountains. It is an evergreen plant about 1 to 2 feet high, with leathery leaves that have their edges rolled under. The saucer-like flowers develop in small clusters at the end of red stems. Alpine Laurel contains natural toxins poisonous to humans.

Fireweed *Epilobium angustifolium (Evening Primrose family)*

Fireweed gets its name from the fact that it quickly invades areas of burned forest and because its tall, bright flowering stalk resembles a flame. Fireweed grows up to 6 feet tall or more, with the lower flowers blooming before the upper ones. Tufts of long, silky hair attached to the seeds carry them on the wind and spread them rapidly to new areas.

Spotted Coralroot *Corallhiza maculata (Orchid family)*

Look for this delicate little orchid on the floor of the Lodgepole Pine forest, growing in the decaying leaves and organic matter. It has no green leaves, and must gather nutrients from tree roots and fungi living underground. The upper petals are reddish in color, and the lower petal is white with dark red spots. Pale yellow albino plants, with white flowers and no spots, occasionally occur.

Subalpine Spirea *Spirea splendens (Rose family)*

This branching shrub, with its soft-looking pink flower heads in dense clusters, grows beside mountain streams and can be up to 4 feet tall. The flowers are very small but are so close together that the clusters appear to be larger flowers. Leaves grow alternately on the stem and are toothed.

Pink and Red Flowers, continued

Lewis Monkeyflower *Mimulus lewisii (Figwort family)*

Monkeyflowers are snapdragon-looking flowers that live in moist areas, especially along the small streams of the Tetons. They are easily identified with their five rose-pink petals that form a funnel and two bright yellow patches in the throat of the funnel. Monkeyflowers often hang over the water or live in the spray of tumbling streams.

Red Mountainheath *Phyllodoce empetriformis (Heath family)*

Mountainheath is a small, evergreen shrub growing in low clumps and mats, with pineneedle-like leaves. It is common around the shores of mountain lakes. The flowers are bright pink, urn shaped, and hang down from long, slender stalks. It is closely related to the heath plants of Europe.

Rose Pussytoes *Antennaria microphylla (Composite family)*

This little plant grows in dry, open sites in the lower mountains and moraines. Pussytoes forms a low, spreading, gray-green plant with flowering stems reaching up to 12 inches high. The flowers are each only about ⅛ inch across and grow in heads resembling a cat's paw. The actual flowers are inconspicuous and have no ray flowers, but the pink or red bracts look like the flower.

Moss Campion *Silene acaulis (Pink family)*

Moss Campion grows high in the mountains, where it forms a dense cushion-like mat a foot or more across and only a few inches high. Numerous tiny pink flowers, each only ¼ inch across, cover the plant. Campion grows in rocky soil and on talus slopes and flowers in the latter part of the summer.

Elephanthead *Pedicularis groenlandica (Figwort family)*

The corolla of this unique flower forms the shape of an elephant's head with upturned trunk and ears, making it unmistakable. Elephanthead grows in densely flowered spikes and is common in moist meadows and around alpine lakes. The spikes are roughly 8 to 24 inches tall.

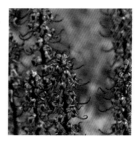

Skyrocket Gilia *Ipomopsis aggregata (Phlox family)*

The bright scarlet flowers of Skyrocket stand out in the sagebrush flats and open woods where they grow. The plant is 1 to 3 feet tall, with clusters of brilliant, trumpet-shaped flowers. A biennial plant, it only produces a small clump of basal leaves the first year. The second year it flowers and dies. The leaves are deeply dissected.

Indian Paintbrush *Castilleja miniata (Figwort Family)*

This paintbrush species prefers the moist meadows of the woods along trails and into the canyons. A similar species, growing in the sagebrush, is the state flower of Wyoming. All paintbrushes have colorful bracts that appear as the flower, and all are parasitic on other plants' roots. A dozen different paintbrush species inhabit the park.

Narrowleaf Collomia *Collomia linearis (Phlox family)*

Look for this little flower on moraines and sage-brush flats in early summer. The stem is about 12 inches tall with long, narrow leaves. Numerous clusters of pink, tubular flowers at the top of the plant are surrounded by large, leafy green bracts.

Wildfire

Wildfire is a natural and dynamic process, important to the health of the park's plants and animals. Some plants have adapted to periodic fires and rely on them to re-sprout from roots or to open their cones for seed dispersal.

Animals then benefit from the new growth. Wildflowers in particular seem to thrive during the years after a wildfire.

Every year Grand Teton National Park experiences wildfires ignited by lightning. Some of these fires are allowed to burn while others are fought and extinguished. In general, the park fire policy is to suppress naturally caused fires that threaten irreplaceable natural and cultural resources. However, fires that occur in other areas may be monitored, managed, and allowed to burn for a time. Wildfires may occur in forests, sagebrush flats, or grasslands.

Fire contributes to the park's ecosystem by opening up the soil to sunlight, enriching it with nitrogen from the ash, and providing an opportunity for less competitive plants to grow. In areas dominated by one species, such as the Lodgepole Pine forest or sagebrush flats, fire re-starts the natural progression of plants with new shoots of grasses, shrubs, wildflowers, and tree seedlings.

Indian Paintbrush (right)

Blue and Purple Flowers

Hairy Clematis *Clematis hirsutissima (Buttercup family)*

Also commonly known as Sugarbowl, this dull purple flower grows in canyon meadows and in open areas of forest and sagebrush. The single flowers are about an inch long, shaped like a sugarbowl, and nod over at the end of the stem. Clematis grows in clusters about 1 to 2 feet tall. Fine white hair covers the plant, which blooms in early summer.

Rock Clematis *Clematis occidentalis (Buttercup family)*

Rock Clematis is a climbing vine, with leaf stalks that twine themselves around other plants. Like the Hairy Clematis, this flower has colored sepals but doesn't actually develop true petals. The flowers are 2 to 3 inches broad, and the vine may reach 10 feet in height. When the flowers go to seed, long, feathery plumes carry the seeds in the wind. Clematis grows in shaded forest, usually on steep slopes.

Pasqueflower *Anenome multifida (Buttercup family)*

Pasqueflower is a lovely spring flower growing in low clusters in moist forest meadows, not long after the snow melts. It looks somewhat like Sugarbowl, but is larger and often upright rather than nodding. Also, the Sugarbowl's leaves grow opposite each other and Pasqueflower's leaves, which are only at the base of the plant, do not. Pasqueflower is covered with long, silky hairs.

Blue Penstemon *Penstemon cyaneus (Figwort family)*

A dozen different penstemons inhabit the park, and they range in color from deep blue to pale lavendar. All have a similar appearance, having clusters of tube-shaped flowers each with a pro-truding, beard-like stamen. This gives them the common name of Beardstongue. They all general-ly prefer dry, open ground.

Wild Blue Flax (previous pages)

Low Larkspur *Delphinium nuttallianum (Buttercup family)*

Larkspur inhabits the sagebrush flats and lower hills of the park during early summer. A taller larkspur blooms later in the summer, but both display the characteristic "spur" on one of the five purple sepals enclosing the four lighter colored petals. Low Larkspur stands about 8 to 12 inches tall, and each plant produces up to ten flowers. Larkspur is highly poisonous to grazing animals.

Duncecap Larkspur *Delphinium occidentale*
(Buttercup Family)

Blooming in mid to late summer, Duncecap Larkspur has five colored, petal-like sepals, with one forming a long spur that makes the flower look like a pointed cap. There are four petals as well. Duncecap is easily identified by its thick stem that may reach 6 feet high.

Showy Fleabane *Erigeron speciosus (Composite family)*

Several similar-looking plants grow in the park, but this one has up to 12 flower heads on long stems, with each flower about an inch across and having many narrow, whitish to light blue rays. The center disk is bright yellow-orange. Showy Fleabane has smooth-edged leaves growing the full length of its stems and grows along trails in open wooded areas in the lower elevations.

Fringed Gentian *Gentiana detonsa (Iris family)*

Although it isn't widespread in the park, the 6 inch tall Fringed Gentian is worth looking for. Often found in meadows close to the roads, especially near Jackson Lake Dam, its tubular purple flowers have delicately fringed edges. Its green, pointed sepals have a sharp, boat-like keel.

Blue and Purple Flowers, continued

Alpine Aster *Aster alpigenus (Composite family)*

There's no confusing this aster with others, since it's usually found high in the mountains, in a crack in the rock. Like other alpine flowers it stays low to the ground. One flower per stem and long, narrow leaves arising from the base of the stem help identify it. The inner disk is made up of numerous tiny yellow flowers, each with five petals.

Thickstem Aster *Aster integrifolius (Composite family)*

This variety of aster is fairly easy to identify as it blooms very late in the summer, has thick stems covered with gland-like hairs near the top, and has several flower heads on each stem. Large clasping leaves surround the stem. The flower has fewer rays than the other asters and can look more ragged. The disk flowers are orangish yellow.

Mountain Townsendia *Townsendia alpigena (Sunflower family)*

As its name implies, this flower lives on the high slopes and mountain ridges. It grows close to the ground with one flower on each short stem. The flower heads are about ½ inch across and usually bloom in late summer. The leaves of Mountain Townsendia are covered with fine hair and are curled into a spoon shape.

Common Blue-eyed Grass *Sisyrinchium idahoense (Iris family)*

Blue-eyed Grass is a small iris that grows in moist soil along streams or in shaded meadows. Its flattened stem reaches 6 to 12 inches in height, with up to five flowers on each stem. There are three petals and two sepals, each with a tiny point on the end, making up the purple iris flower.

Giant Hyssop *Agastache urticofolia (Mint Family)*

Also known as the Nettle-leaved Horse-mint, this tall plant has the typical square stems and opposite leaves of the Mint family. Giant Hyssop is common in moraine meadows along the base of the mountains. It is used in herbal medicine for a variety of ailments.

Harebell *Campanula rotundifolia (Bluebell family)*

Harebell is a delicate flower found in pine and fir forests and along trails and road cuts in the park. The plant is about 1 to 2 feet tall with numerous flowers hanging down from slender stems. The unopened buds are erect. In dry soil the plant may be shorter, with just one flower. Harebell has rounded leaves at the base and narrow pointed leaves on the stems.

Mountain Bluebell *Mertensia ciliata (Borage family)*

Bluebell is a leafy plant with small bunches of drooping, light blue flowers. The buds are a light purple and turn blue as they open. The bluebell plant grows large and full, with numerous flowers, and blooms in midsummer. Common along streams in the lower mountains and moraines, Mountain Bluebell is utilized by many animals.

Silver Lupine *Lupinus argenteus (Pea family)*

Lupine grows in colorful patches in the sagebrush flats, meadows, and in more open areas of the Lodgepole Pine forest. Like other members of the pea family, it has irregular flowers growing in dense racemes at top of the stem. Lupine's leaves are made of thin leaflets that spread out like an open hand. At times, various parts of the plant are poisonous.

Blue and Purple Flowers, continued

Columbia Monkshood *Aconitum columbianum* *(Buttercup family)*

Monkshood is a conspicuous, deep purple flower often seen in the foothills and lower canyons where the trail crosses a small stream. It may grow to be five or six feet tall, and blooms most of the summer. Two of the sepals form a hood containing the two small petals, giving the flower its name.

Blue Violet *Viola adunca (Violet family)*

These pansy-looking little flowers bloom during the first half of summer, in moist soil and usually in the shade. They aren't abundant, but can show up anywhere from the valley floor to near timberline. The lower petal has a conspicuous, hooked spur. When the flowers first appear they seem to have no stem, but as the flower matures it may grow to 6 or 8 inches.

Blue Camas *Camassia quamash (Lily family)*

This early summer lily grows in moist areas of the valley, especially in wet meadows around the larger lakes. It stands out with its 18-inch leafless stalk and cluster of large blue flowers along the top of the stem. Blue Camas has wide, grass-like leaves rising from the base of the plant. Native Americans prized its nutritious bulbs.

Silky Phacelia *Phacelia sericea (Waterleaf family)*

Phacelia is a member of the waterleaf family that lives in dry soil. Phacelia flowers develop very long stamens that stick out of the tiny individual flowers like purple hairs. Silky, silvery hairs cover the stems and leaves. Phacelia grows up to 2 feet tall, with its leaves deeply divided into segments.

Wild Blue Flax *Linum lewisii (Flax family)*

Blue flax is a bright little five-petaled flower as fragile as it is beautiful. The one-inch wide flowers cling to very slender stems which move with the slightest breeze, and they begin to drop their petals within days of opening. Blue flax grows in dry rocky soil, but not in great numbers. Stems of flax species are thin but are tough and fibrous and were used by Native Americans for making string.

Alpine Forget-me-not *Eritrichium nanum (Borage family)*

Growing in a dense cushion high in the mountains, this brilliant little flower exhibits all the survival traits of an alpine plant. It is dwarfed, with long hairs on the stem and leaves to help conserve water, and its distinct flowers attract pollinators during the brief summer. This is the official flower of Grand Teton National Park.

Sky Pilot *Polemonium viscosum (Phlox family)*

Sky Pilot blooms in the second half of summer, high in the mountains. Its purple, funnel-shaped blossoms have orange anthers, and the leaves are up to 6 inches long and are divided into numerous leaflets. One identifying characteristic of Sky Pilot and other plants of this genus, such as Jacob's Ladder, is a strong, skunky odor.

Mountain Bog Gentian *Gentiana calycosa (Gentian family)*

Although it isn't widespread, this flower is often encountered along the canyon trails, especially on the banks of mountain streams. It grows about 6 to 12 inches tall and has a single deep-blue flower at the top of the stem. The funnel-shaped flower is about 1.5 inches long, with five lobes, and between each lobe protrudes a short, blue point. Smooth leaves grow on opposite sides of the stem.

Berries and Their Flowers

Highbush Huckleberry *Vaccinium membranaceum*

The popular Huckleberry has small, globe-shaped pink and white flowers that mature into purple fruit. It is common along most of the trails through Lodgepole Pine forests.

Utah Honeysuckle *Vaccinium membranaceum*

Also known as Red Twinberry, it has a pair of white, funnel-shaped flowers with a bulbous base. The fruit also comes in pairs and is bright red.

Bearberry Honeysuckle *Lonicera involverata*

This honeysuckle also grows twin flowers and fruit, but a bract surrounds the base of the Bearberry flower, and the fruit is blackish purple.

Baneberry *Actaea rubra*

The clusters of white Baneberry flowers turn into either white or red berries that are considered poisonous.

Mountain Ash *Sorbus scopulina*

Large, white clusters of Mountain Ash flowers turn into thick bunches of bright orange berries. They are common along the lower trails and moraines.

Chokecherry *Prunus virginiana*

Common Chokecherry grows along many streams and roadsides in the park and has white flowers in long, thin clusters. In August they turn into numerous red fruit.

Black Hawthorn (previous pages)

Bearberry, or Kinnikinnik *Arctostaphylos ura-ursi*

Bearberry is a low, evergreen plant found along the trails in dry Lodgepole Pine forests. American Indians dried and smoked its leaves as a tobacco substitute. The small white flowers mature into red fruit.

Black Elderberry *Sambucus racemosa*

Elderberry flowers are creamy white and grow in dense clusters, and the red fruit hangs in thick bunches.

Western Serviceberry *Amelanchier alnifolia*

Serviceberry has white flowers with five petals, and the dark purple berries are favored by wildlife. It blooms early in the spring.

Buffaloberry *Shepherdia canadensis*

Buffaloberry grows along the Snake River and in the Lodgepole Pine forests. The flowers have no petals and are often missed, but the reddish orange fruit is easy to see.

Redosier Dogwood *Cornus stolonifera*

Dogwood has clusters of tiny white flowers growing on twigs with purplish red bark. Wildlife eat the white fruit.

Oregon Grape *Mahonia repens*

Common along trails over the moraines, this small evergreen shrub has prickly leaves and dense clusters of bright yellow flowers early in the summer. The leaves turn color along with the purple berries.

Berries and Their Flowers, continued

Mountain Snowberry *Symphoricarpos oreophilus*

This shrub has whitish pink flowers that are small and bell-shaped, growing in clusters near the tops of the branches. The white fruit stays on the plant through August.

Spreading Dogbane *Apocynum androssaemifolium*

Common in the Lodgepole Pine forest, this low shrub has bell-shaped, pink striped flowers in clusters. The ripe fruit is red, but was used when still green by Native Americans as a medicine.

Mountain Ash berries

Please Don't Eat the Berries

Some of the park's flowers, especially those of shrubs along the trails, produce berries each summer. Although eating them is legal, they can be confusing to visitors unfamiliar with all the varieties, and they range from delicious to poisonous. If you aren't positive, don't eat it.

Black bear eating serviceberries in the fall (right)

Best Short Walks For Wildflowers

Death Canyon Trailhead to Phelps Lake Overlook

Less than a mile one way, but gradually uphill, this trail begins in a Lodge-pole Pine forest, crosses several meadows with aspen trees, skirts rocks and boulders, and ends up on a high moraine overlooking a lake. Along the way there are many different wildflower habitats, and flowers bloom all summer. Look especially in the cool, shaded areas where the trail crosses streams.

East Shore of Jenny Lake

From the Jenny Lake Parking Area, take the trail that leaves the Boat Dock and follows the east side of the lake, away from the mountains. This trail goes in and out of small clearings as it cuts through a Lodgepole Pine forest. It ends up at String Lake after about three miles of easy walking. This is a good place to find early summer flowers as well as shade-loving flowers later in the summer.

Taggart Lake Loop

From the Taggart Lake Trailhead take the trail to the right to reach the lake, then return on the 2.4 mile path that climbs over the moraine and winds down Beaver Creek. These 4 miles of fairly easy hiking hold lots of variety in vegetation and scenery. The trail goes through dry meadows, along streams, through an area of regrowth after a forest fire, and passes through different kinds of conifer forest. Wildflowers bloom somewhere along this trail all summer.

Cascade Canyon

Cascade Canyon Stream

The easiest way to get into Cascade Canyon is to take the boat shuttle across Jenny Lake, but you can also walk around the west side of the lake to experience a greater variety of flowers. From the West Shore Boat Dock, the trail climbs up through the cool, shaded spruce forest and into the canyon. Hike as far as you want, and return the same way. There are rocky hillsides, subalpine meadows, streams, stands of open forest, and eventually the alpine zone.

Field of Butter and Eggs in front of the Tetons (right)

Selected Weeds and Nonnative Flowers

Oxeye Daisy

Not all of the wildflowers you see in Grand Teton National Park are really wild. A few of them are weeds or exotic flowers that have invaded the natural communities of the park. They often thrive and crowd out native plants, and in some locations may appear to be the dominant species. Several of these exotics are so well established that they are here to stay, and botanists usually include them as a part of the park's flora.

Spotted Knapweed *Centaurae maculosa*

Knapweed is common along roadsides and streambanks, especially in the east side of the park. The plant is 2 to 4 feet tall, with small pinkish purple flowers.

Canada Thistle *Cirsium arrense*

There are two similar looking thistles in the park. Canada Thistle is generally not as tall as Musk Thistle, and its flower head has bracts that are spineless.

Musk Thistle *Carduus nutans*

Musk Thistle grows up to 6 feet tall and can form dense stands in open fields. The flower head has long, spine tipped bracts below it.

Salsify *Tragopogon dubius*

This 1 to 3-foot-tall weed has pale yellow flowers with long green bracts extending past the petals. It looks like a large dandelion when it goes to seed.

Common Dandelion *Taraxacum officinale*

This familiar weed grows in abundance in the former agricultural land in the eastern part of the park. In June it can color entire meadows.

Oxeye Daisy *Chrysanthemum leucanthemum*

Oxeye Daisy is a cultivated white sunflower that has gotten into the wild. It grows about 1 to 2 feet tall, with numerous stems and a single flower on each. It inhabits roadsides and the edges of parking areas.

Common Tansy *Tanacetum vulgare*

Tansy grows from 1 to 6 feet tall, with clusters of button-like yellow flowers. It is a member of the sunflower family that has escaped from cultivation.

Butter and Eggs *Linaria dalmatica*

This roadside and meadow weed blooms in mid-summer throughout the park. The plant is 1 to 2 feet tall, with yellow and orange flowers resembling snapdragons.

Index and Checklist

- ❏ Arnica, Heartleaf 21
- ❏ Ash, Mountain 46
- ❏ Aster, Alpine 40
- ❏ Aster, Engelmann 13
- ❏ Aster, Thickstem 40
- ❏ Balsamroot, Arrowleaf 18
- ❏ Baneberry★★ 46
- ❏ Bearberry★ 47
- ❏ Bedstraw, Northern 14
- ❏ Bistort, American 14
- ❏ Blazing Star Mentzelia★★ 22
- ❏ Bluebell, Mountain 41
- ❏ Blue-eyed Grass, Common★★★ 40
- ❏ Bog-orchid, White 10
- ❏ Buckwheat, Sulfur 12
- ❏ Buffaloberry 47
- ❏ Butter and Eggs 53
- ❏ Buttercup, Sagebrush 19
- ❏ Camas, Blue★★ 42
- ❏ Campion, Moss 32
- ❏ Campion, White 15
- ❏ Chokecherry 46
- ❏ Cinquefoil, Shrubby 20
- ❏ Clematis, Hairy★ 38
- ❏ Clematis, Rock★ 38
- ❏ Collomia, Narrowleaf 33
- ❏ Columbine, Colorado 14
- ❏ Columbine, Yellow 22
- ❏ Coneflower, Prairie 20
- ❏ Coralroot, Spotted 31
- ❏ Cowparsnip 11
- ❏ Daisy, Oxeye 53
- ❏ Daisy, Wooly 21
- ❏ Dandelion, Common 53
- ❏ Dandelion, Mountain 18
- ❏ Death Camas, Mountain 12
- ❏ Dogbane, Spreading 48
- ❏ Dogwood, Redosier 47
- ❏ Dryas, White★★★ 15
- ❏ Elderberry, Black★★ 47
- ❏ Elephanthead 33
- ❏ Evening Primrose, Tufted★ 15
- ❏ False Solomon Seal 13
- ❏ Fireweed 31
- ❏ Flax, Wild Blue 43
- ❏ Fleabane, Showy 39
- ❏ Forget-me-not, Alpine 43
- ❏ Gentian, Fringed 39
- ❏ Gentian, Mountain Bog 43
- ❏ Gentian, Showy Green 13
- ❏ Geranium, Sticky 28
- ❏ Goldeneye, Showy 21
- ❏ Groundsel, Western 21
- ❏ Harebell 41
- ❏ Hawksbeard, Low 18
- ❏ Hollyhock, Mountain 29
- ❏ Honeysuckle, Bearberry 46
- ❏ Honeysuckle, Utah 46
- ❏ Huckleberry★★★ 46
- ❏ Hyssop, Giant 41
- ❏ Knapweed, Spotted 52
- ❏ Ladies Tresses★ 10
- ❏ Largeflower Hymenoxys★ 23
- ❏ Larkspur, Duncecap 39
- ❏ Larkspur, Low 39
- ❏ Laurel, Alpine★ 31
- ❏ Lily, Glacier 23
- ❏ Lily, Leopard★ 23
- ❏ Lily, Sego★★ 10
- ❏ Lupine, Silver 41
- ❏ Marigold, Marsh★ 13
- ❏ Monkeyflower, Lewis 32
- ❏ Monkeyflower, Yellow 23
- ❏ Monkshood, Columbia 42
- ❏ Mountainheath, Red★★ 32
- ❏ Mules Ear, White 12
- ❏ Mules-ear Wyethia 18
- ❏ One-flower Helianthella 19
- ❏ Orchid, Calypso★ 30
- ❏ Oregon Grape 47
- ❏ Paintbrush, Indian 33
- ❏ Paintbrush, Sulfur 24
- ❏ Parnassia, Rocky Mountain 14
- ❏ Parsley, Desert 19
- ❏ Pasqueflower★ 38
- ❏ Penstemon, Blue 38
- ❏ Phacelia, Silky 42
- ❏ Phlox, Longleaf 29

- [ ] Phlox, Many-flowered 10
- [ ] Pondlily, Rocky Mountain 22
- [ ] Prairiesmoke 28
- [ ] Primrose, Parry* 30
- [ ] Pussytoes, Rose 32
- [ ] Rabbitbrush 20
- [ ] Rose, Wild 28
- [ ] Salsify 53
- [ ] Serviceberry, Western 47
- [ ] Shooting Star 29
- [ ] Sky Pilot** 43
- [ ] Skyrocket Gilia 33
- [ ] Snowberry, Mountain** 48
- [ ] Snowbrush Ceanothus 15
- [ ] Spirea, Subalpine 31
- [ ] Spring Beauty 28
- [ ] St. Johnwort, Western 24
- [ ] Steershead* 29
- [ ] Stonecrop, Lanceleaved 24
- [ ] Strawberry, Woodland 11
- [ ] Sunflower, Nodding Little 20
- [ ] Sweetvetch, Northern 30
- [ ] Tansy, Common** 53
- [ ] Thimbleberry 12
- [ ] Thistle, Canada 52
- [ ] Thistle, Musk 53
- [ ] Townsendia, Mountain 40
- [ ] Twinflower, Northern* 30
- [ ] Violet, Blue* 42
- [ ] Violet, Yellow 19
- [ ] Yampah 11
- [ ] Yarrow, Common 11
- [ ] Yellow Bell** 22

* Photograph by Elizabeth Boehm and Fred Pflughoft Stock Photo
** Photograph by Leon Tuten
*** Photograph by Frank C. Craighead (also bottom three fire aftermath photos, p.34)

©2005 Grand Teton Natural History Association
Grand Teton National Park
P.O. Box 170, Moose WY 83012
www.grandtetonpark.org

Design and Production by
Jeff Pollard Design & Associates

Maps by
Mike Reagan

Project Coordinated by
Jan Lynch, Executive Director,
Grand Teton Natural History Association

Printed by
Paragon Press

ISBN 0-931895-61-8